All About Sand

By John Samar
Art by Mihailo Tatic

Library For All Ltd.

Library For All is an Australian not for profit organisation with a mission to make knowledge accessible to all via an innovative digital library solution.
Visit us at www.libraryforall.org.au

All About Sand

First published 2019

Published by Library For All Ltd
Email: info@libraryforall.org.au
URL: http://www.libraryforall.org.au

This work is licensed under the Creative Commons Attribution-NonCommercial-NoDerivatives 4.0 International License. To view a copy of this license, visit http://creativecommons.org/licenses/by-nc-nd/4.0/.

This book was produced by the Together For Education Partnership supported by the Australian Government through the Papua New Guinea-Australia Partnership.

Original illustrations by Mihailo Tatic

All About Sand
Samar, John
ISBN: 978-1-925986-22-8

How much do you know about sand?

Sand is found on the beach and riverbanks.

People visit beaches to swim and rest on the sand.

Sand gets very hot in the sun.

Children make sand castles on the beach.

Sand is used to make glass.

Sand is used to make bricks for houses.

Sand is used to mix cement to build houses.

Sand is found in deserts all over the world.

A sand storm in the desert can hurt people's eyes.

Sand barriers stop erosion of beaches.

There are many things to learn about sand!

Did you enjoy this book?

We have hundreds more expertly curated original stories to choose from.

We work in partnership with authors, educators, cultural advisors, governments and NGOs to bring the joy of reading to children everywhere.

Did you know?

We create global impact in these fields by embracing the United Nations Sustainable Development Goals.

libraryforall.org.au

About the contributors

John Mier Samar comes from the East Sepik Province. He is a multi-skilled communications expert. He was one of the first batches of PNG Journalists to be trained at the University of Papua New Guinea in 1975. John is an accomplished photographer and an author. His photographs have been published in some major publications in the Pacific.

John is not new to writing and has printed a few books and newsletters such as *'A Public Relations Handbook for Managers in Papua New Guinea'* and *'Ok Tedi – The Future – Ok Tedi bai igo we nau?'.* At age 8, John started reading English comics then moved onto Australian newspapers such as the Courier Mail, The Australian, Time Magazine and Newsweek. John had been fortunate to attend a week's course for Children's book writing, which was conducted by Buk Bilong Pikinini in Port Moresby, 2011. John has since then put his creative flair for imagination into writing.

CPSIA information can be obtained
at www.ICGtesting.com
Printed in the USA
BVHW022151141121
621668BV00017B/504